reflections
ON FAITH & PRAYER

reflections
ON FAITH & PRAYER

JOSEPH S. CARROLL

School of Biblical Training

AMBASSADOR INTERNATIONAL
GREENVILLE, SOUTH CAROLINA & BELFAST, NORTHERN IRELAND

www.ambassador-international.com

Reflections on Faith and Prayer
Copyright © 2013 EI School of Biblical Training

The content of this book was written by Joseph Carroll.

Scripture quotations are from the King James Version.

All rights reserved

Printed in the United States of America

ISBN: 978-1-62020-221-0
eISBN: 978-1-62020-319-4

Author photo: Pat Rawlins
Cover design: Elly Kalagayan
Typesetting: Bethany Cook
E-book conversion: Anna Riebe

AMBASSADOR INTERNATIONAL
Emerald House
427 Wade Hampton Blvd.
Greenville, SC 29609, USA
www.ambassador-international.com

AMBASSADOR BOOKS
The Mount
2 Woodstock Link
Belfast, BT6 8DD, Northern Ireland, UK
www.ambassadormedia.co.uk

The colophon is a trademark of Ambassador

This book is dedicated
to all those who are true
worshipers of Jesus Christ.

Endorsements

Here is truth and insight to enrich your faith and prayer! These pages will remind you of lessons once learned and established and serve as a source of fresh motivation to move from thoughts and good intentions about prayer to actually praying!

— Pastor Bob Davis

This book holds gems from the heart of a man who walked before God. Mr. Carroll was a man who worshiped Jesus Christ, and the fragrance of his intimacy with Christ is expressed in words in this booklet. This verse could describe Mr. Carroll's labor in the gospel: "…men ought always to pray and not faint" (Luke 18:1). I heard Mr. Carroll say often: "Prayer and the Word of God are fuel for the fire of faith." Another common quote was, "The Christian walks on two feet in the path of obedience: surrender and faith." Mr. Carroll was a man who modeled the life of faith.

— Wallace Francis
USA National Director of Ambassadors for Christ

Contents

Foreword
Introduction
How to Use This Book

Month One
Faith

Month Two
Prayer

Foreword

As our family visited with Joseph Carroll in the late 1960's, I listened to his vision for a Christian training school. We were standing on the road, gazing across the empty field which would later become The Evangelical Institute campus, when Mr. Carroll said to me, "I can now see the first building." On that cool summer evening, I saw only what was before me--a field against a canopy of trees. Mr. Carroll, however, looked with the eyes of faith and saw what the Lord had planted in his heart through much prayer. This experience, when only a young pastor, introduced to me the biblical way of faith.

Biblical faith is trusting God specifically and implicitly for what He reveals in His Word and through prayer. Faith is the way God accomplishes His will through us for the furthering of His kingdom and the honoring of His Name. It is His appointed way for His heavenly will to become our earthly reality. I had never known a man who spoke of faith as Mr. Carroll spoke. I had never known another man who lived by faith as Mr. Carroll lived, to whom faith was not an abstract, nebulous attitude, as I was accustomed to thinking. For Mr. Carroll, faith was living, dynamic, and absolutely necessary in life and ministry.

Prayer and obedience, of course, are inseparably joined to faith. As my relationship with Mr. Carroll continued over the years,

I heard him frequently emphasize the core truths of prayer, obedience, and faith as necessary for walking with God.

These excerpts on faith and prayer come from Mr. Carroll's sermons and lectures. Their brevity makes them useful in personal devotions and small groups. The truths he shares are vitally important and should be read again and again. Once will not suffice, for we must meditate on God's truths in order to make precise applications in our lives.

Faith and prayer should become to your spiritual life what breathing is to your body.

Pastor Jerald (Jerry) R. White, Jr.

Introduction

No one knew the Lord like His twelve disciples. Day after day, they observed His life in detail, which led them to two basic requests: "Lord, increase our faith"; "Lord, teach us to pray." These men wanted their lives to also reflect the key elements of faith and prayer they witnessed in Jesus.

In one of the entries in this book, Mr. Carroll refers to David's walk with God. He says that David was no theorist. I had the privilege of working alongside Joseph Carroll for almost thirty years. I can say the same thing of him. He was no theorist when it came to living by faith and maintaining a prayer life. For him, faith and prayer were essential for daily living. He constantly studied with a view to improving his mastery of these two vital areas.

In the school of discipleship Mr. Carroll founded, these two subjects were woven into the fabric of all that was taught. He believed that unless these skills were instilled into the core of each graduate's soul, our teaching had failed.

The devotional book you have in your hands is comprised of excerpts gleaned from Mr. Carroll's thirty years of ministry at the EI School of Biblical Training. One month of devotionals is devoted to faith and another to prayer. These selections are meant to inspire your pursuit of the Lord by providing insights from the heart of one man who walked this very path.

This book is a testimony to Mr. Carroll's teaching and his life. Those who heard him speak will recognize much of the material. We trust these daily readings will serve to bring back thoughts of the larger context in which they were spoken. For those who never heard him, the selections should challenge your life, as well as help you sense the spirit of a man who made God his ultimate goal.

My prayer is that the instruction of Hebrews 13:7 will become a reality for each reader: *Remember those who led you, who spoke the word of God to you; considering the result of their conduct, imitate their faith.*

Art Nuernberg
Pastoral Director of the EI School of Biblical Training

How To Use This Book

This small volume has been compiled as a source of inspiration for God's true servants. The selections were chosen to assist you in contemplating what it means to have a vibrant, joyous prayer life and in deepening your understanding of the life of faith.

Reading God's Word and spending time alone with Him in fellowship and worship is a great joy! These reflections are meant to support your meditations on the Scriptures. Each morning or evening, we hope you will use this book to allow the Lord to refresh and settle your heart before Him. As each week ends, you will have the opportunity to write what the Lord has taught you on the pages provided.

Eternal life is to KNOW God and His son, Jesus Christ. May this brief work prove useful as you continue your pursuit of Him.

Colin Brazier
General Director of the EI School of Biblical Training

To stretch my hand and touch Him,
Though He be far away;
To raise my eyes and see Him
Through darkness and through day;
To lift my voice and call Him -
This is to pray!

Month 1

*Faith is not an intellectual assent.
It is the absolute surrender of self
to the will of God, who has a right to
command this surrender.*

— Bishop Lightfoot

How Good is the God We Adore

How good is the God we adore,
Our faithful, unchangeable Friend;
His love is as great as His power,
And knows neither measure nor end.

'Tis Jesus, the first and the last,
Whose Spirit shall guide us safe home;
We'll praise Him for all that is past,
We'll trust Him for all that's to come.

J. Hart

Day 1   CARES AND BURDENS

Casting all your care upon him; for he careth for you (I Peter 5:7).
Be careful for nothing...(Philippians 4:6).

Are you fretting? Anxious? Frustrated? Are you carrying burdens you were never built to bear?

Hudson Taylor had a plaque on the wall of his office, which read:

> Bear not a single care thyself;
> One is too much for thee.
> The work is Mine, and Mine alone,
> Thy work, to rest in Me.

"Bear not a single care thyself." Are you care-worn? If so, you are out of the will of God. *Casting all your care upon him; for he careth for you*. Notice that it is ALL of your cares. Why? Because He cares for you. He wants to bear your cares.

Why do we remain burdened with cares? Very often, it is simply unbelief. We have never committed our care to the Lord, leaving the matter to His control, believing Him to order every detail. Faith brings us to rest. "Thy work, to rest in Me."

The Word of God speaks to our unbelief: *Be careful for nothing* or *in nothing be anxious*. Anxiety denies our heavenly Father's

Day 1   CARES AND BURDENS
(continued)

care.

At any given moment of time, you are either trusting the Lord or you are trusting yourself. You have either committed your care to the Lord or you have committed yourself and your resources to the need.

The God who created this universe and the universes beyond this universe is pleased by faith, which commits every care to Him.

Reflections on Faith

Day 2   EXPECTANT FAITH

...my expectation is from Him (Psalm 62:5).

When I visited Westminster Abbey, I was surprised to see a wooden lectern in memory of the great Baptist and pioneer of faith, William Carey. *Attempt great things for God* was inscribed in gold letters on the front of his lectern. I knew this was only part of Carey's great statement of faith. Where was the rest? I moved behind the lectern and read: *Expect great things from God.* This gold lettering was in shadow. The light shone only on the portion which spoke of attempting great things. There was no spotlight on his expectation.

Carey was a man of vibrant, confident, expectant faith who always attempted great things for God and always expected great things of God; therefore, he was greatly used.

If there is one deficiency in the lives of Christians who truly desire to please God, it is a lack of expectation. Are you really expecting God to work? Are you expecting God to answer your prayers?

Reflections on Faith

Day 3   DO NOT FRET

Fret not thyself because of evildoers, neither be thou envious against the workers of iniquity. For they shall soon be cut down like the grass, and wither as the green herb. Trust in the Lord, and do good; so shalt thou dwell in the land, and verily thou shalt be fed. Delight thyself also in the Lord; and he shall give thee the desires of thine heart. Commit thy way unto the Lord; trust also in him; and he shall bring it to pass (Psalm 37:1-5).

When David penned this Psalm, he was an old man writing from his rich experiences in proving God's faithfulness. He was not a theorist as he spoke of a life of faith. David didn't understand why the people he thought should be punished were prospering. From this very deep experience, he directed three times, *Fret not*. The meaning of "fret" is "coming to anger." If you fret, getting disturbed and upset, you may become resentful and bitter, which grieves the Spirit of God.

Trust in the Lord, whatever the situation. He IS the answer. He can completely turn the situation. How do you trust in the Lord? You have faith in the faithfulness of God, never faith in your faith. His faithfulness never alters.

Dwell in the land, and verily thou shalt be fed. The Lord cares for His own. Believe and have faith in the faithfulness of God.

Day 3   DO NOT FRET
(continued)

Delight thyself also in the Lord. David concentrated on nurturing his love for the Lord. He delighted in God, finding satisfaction and joy in this relationship. David committed himself to look to the Lord.

Live by faith in your heavenly Father to provide all your needs. Live by faith in the Lord Jesus Christ, cultivating your love for Him, developing a life of intimacy that satisfies the deepest needs of your heart. Live by faith in the Holy Spirit to strengthen and guide you. Walk each day trusting and delighting in the triune God, and you will not fret.

Day 4 — ACT OF FAITH

The Lord is my Shepherd...(Psalm 23:1).

David was a great king, a great leader, a great psalmist. What was the key to his greatness? There came a time when he made a total commitment to God; without which, he would never have come to a true knowledge of the Lord.

Very early in his life, while minding sheep, David made a discovery. This lad understood that he was a sheep in need of a shepherd. David knew sheep to be helpless and foolish by nature and obviously realized that he too had made foolish mistakes. Jeremiah proclaimed that it is not possible for man to direct his steps. No matter the man's intellect, experience, or gifts, he needs a shepherd.

In response to this revelation, David very simply expressed his commitment in a psalm. He wrote: *The Lord is my shepherd.* David's use of "my" made it personal. In an act of faith, he totally committed himself to the Lord as his present-tense Shepherd. He was saying, "I am committed to the Lord as my Shepherd, to be a sheep in His pasture. Because I am under God's total authority, I no longer belong to myself."

Reflections on Faith

Day 5 — ACT OF FAITH

...I shall not want (Psalm 23:1).

Now that David was under the care of the Shepherd, he could declare: *I shall not want*. David had entrusted himself to the Shepherd to provide for him and to protect him. He would look only to one Person for the rest of his life. Therefore, he would never want for provision at any time. Neither would he want for protection. These words, *I shall not want*, were proof of David's total commitment.

When did you give yourself totally to Jesus Christ? When did you become His sheep, living by faith in Him to protect you and be your Source of provision all the days of your life? When did you become a servant-sheep under His control, wonderfully under the care of your Shepherd 24 hours a day?

Day 6   ATTITUDE OF FAITH

He maketh me to lie down...he leadeth me...(Psalm 23:2).

When an attitude of faith follows your act of faith, God takes over: *He maketh me to lie down....* Why does God make David lie down? He wants to lead him: *He leadeth me.* It is wonderful to be led by the Lord. Watching God work becomes your life experience.

A sheep will not lie down until it is satisfied. If frightened or in need, it moves. Because David lies down and rests, we know an attitude of faith is operating.

Not until you are lying down is God going to speak to you: *He leadeth me.* You must be still to hear His voice; otherwise, you will be too disturbed, too distressed, too upset, too preoccupied to hear.

Guidance is received when you are still. God's impressions are made when you are quietly resting.

Day 7   ATTITUDE OF FAITH

He maketh me to lie down...he leadeth me...(Psalm 23:2).

God called Moses to the top of a mountain and then let him sit for six days. Six days! Moses was a very busy man. He was the leader of a nation, yet he sat and waited for six days. Any active man finds it very difficult to do nothing for even an hour. Such a man is occupied with his responsibilities.

Moses sat for six long days on the mountain top. God doesn't make mistakes. Did He call Moses days before He wanted to speak to him? No. It took six days for this leader to become quiet, quiet enough to hear the Lord's voice. God spoke to Moses on the seventh day. He waited until Moses was lying down.

Do you have a multitude of problems? If you do, you have chosen to have them. Choose to lie down in an attitude of faith.

Personal Reflections:

Day 8   ATTITUDE OF FAITH

...he leadeth me beside the still waters (Psalm 23:2).

How does God lead? He leads beside waters of stillness; He leads in peacefulness.

How do you know when the Lord is leading you? If you are trusting, you are resting; if you are resting, you are trusting. The evidence of trust *IS* rest. If you are agitated and upset, you are not trusting. When you are trusting, agitatation leaves. You are not disturbed. You are not upset. You find rest.

When I would be waiting to speak at a church meeting or missionary gathering, the Lord would often ask, "Are you trusting?"

"Yes, of course, Lord," I would reply.

"Well, why are you so tense?" My shoulders would drop an inch or two as the tension released. I wasn't trusting; therefore, I wasn't resting.

Rest is the evidence of trust. He leads me beside waters of stillness.

Reflections on Faith

Day 9   ATTITUDE OF FAITH

...he leadeth me beside the still waters (Psalm 23:2).

Anybody who walks with the Lord knows He never shouts. He never raises His voice. His is a still, small voice.

He is a present-tense Shepherd who speaks to remind you that He is always with you. Do you hear His still, small voice? Is the Lord your Shepherd?

When I am still, quiet, believing, and resting, God speaks. What father does not want to speak to his child? What shepherd does not want to guide his sheep?

"Oh, but I have other plans." Forget about your plans. God does not need your ideas. Instead, say, "What do You want me to do, Lord?" Understanding will follow.

David heard the still, small voice of the Lord, then wrote his wonderful psalms of faith.

Day 10 ATTITUDE OF FAITH

...he leadeth me in the paths of righteousness for his name's sake
(Psalm 23:3).

There have been times in my life when I have wondered, "Why has God permitted this? Was it for my sake?" As I grew spiritually, I understood that God is perfect in all His ways. All that has happened along my path has been for His glory. That difficult trial, that seemingly impossible circumstance, that suffering I judged to be so unnecessary were all for His glory. He led my steps *for His name's sake*.

Sheep need only one shepherd who makes the decisions. You are helpless to become what God would have you become unless the Shepherd leads you for His own glory and for your fulfillment.

Do you obediently follow the voice of the Shepherd because you believe that He is perfect in all His ways? Who determines the course of your life?

Reflections on Faith

Day 11   AUTHORITY

For unto us a child is born, unto us a son is given: and the government shall be upon his shoulder...(Isaiah 9:6).

Government speaks of three things: authority, responsibility, and the ordering of every detail.

In the British army, an officer's rank is known by the epaulet on his shoulder. Every officer has authority. To determine how much authority, you look at his shoulder. His rank also tells you his level of responsibility. He has responsibility to order the details of the lives of those under his authority.

In 1956, I was introduced to a remarkable, 80 year-old woman with dancing eyes. She was the founder and director of the Door of Hope Mission in Shanghai. Miss Dieterle had to be evacuated to the States after the Communist take over. The Lord then called her to begin a similar work in Taipei.

Some years later, the Southern Baptists on Formosa invited my wife and me to minister in their churches and seminary. This made it possible for me to get to know Miss Dieterle very well. As a German teenager, she came to the realization that the life she was to live had to be a life of faith. When she read Isaiah 9:6, she took it as her life verse. Everything that came to her, no matter what it was, she would say, "Government upon Your shoulders, Lord."

Day 11   AUTHORITY
(continued)

With great authority comes great responsibility. As Miss Dieterle placed the government upon the Lord's shoulder, she was saying, "Now, Lord, the government of this situation is yours. The authority and responsibility are yours. You must order every detail."

As she continued this practice, Miss Dieterle developed amazing faith, which was the key to her remarkable life.

Reflections on Faith

Day 12   AUTHORITY

For unto us a child is born, unto us a son is given: and the government shall be upon his shoulder...(Isaiah 9:6).

During the Japanese occupation of Shanghai, Miss Dieterle was responsible for hundreds of orphans with only a little money trickling in from Germany. One day, her assistant said, "Miss Dieterle, we only have a few bars of soap for our 500 girls." Miss Dieterle had all the girls and staff gather to pray, "Lord, this is an emergency. We are placing the government upon Your shoulders. The responsibility is Yours to provide soap."

As the group was waiting upon the Lord for this need, a Chinese gentleman came to the door inquiring about the ministry. At the conclusion of his tour, he said, "Miss Dieterle, I would like to help you. My funds are tied up by the Japanese, but I am a soap merchant. Perhaps I can help by supplying soap."

This story highlights the simplicity, tenacity, and consistency of Miss Dieterle's faith. As she put the government on the Lord's shoulder, He did wonderful things.

Day 13 — AUTHORITY

For unto us a child is born, unto us a son is given: and the government shall be upon his shoulder...(Isaiah 9:6).

I had unusual liberty every time I ministered in Greenville, South Carolina and became convinced that I was to begin a Bible conference ministry in this city. After three years, I felt the Lord also wanted a Bible school. The Board prayed, "The government is upon Your shoulder, Lord. If You want a school, You must build it."

With 4,000 dollars, we bulldozed an area for a dormitory. I had learned it would cost around 180,000 dollars. We only had enough for the foundation and to lay some blocks.

At this time, a friend invited my family to Florida for a vacation. He said, "I have told my boss about your ministry and he wants to meet you for dinner." I knew this man was shrewd and very wealthy. When we met at the restaurant, he said, "Mr. and Mrs. Carroll, I want to have dinner with your children. You will have dinner with my friends." He took our children to the farthest table in the restaurant. He was going to judge us by our children.

We were about to return to South Carolina when my friend telephoned with news, "My boss wants to contribute to your work. Come by the office." When I arrived, the boss handed me

Day 13 — AUTHORITY
(continued)

a long envelope and said, "Here is some company stock. Do not process it all at once. I am happy to share in your work."

The stock broker who opened the envelope was quite shocked. I, too, was shocked when he told me the stock's value was 250,000 dollars. We had our dormitory.

The Lord only does wondrous things in response to our faith.

Reflections on Faith

Day 14   AUTHORITY

For unto us a child is born, unto us a son is given: and the government shall be upon his shoulder...(Isaiah 9:6).

During our second term in Japan, rents were very, very high. We waited upon the Lord and believed we should build. We found an acceptable spot 70 miles north of Tokyo where I could be satisfied that my wife and children were safe while I traveled. We needed 3,200 dollars.

We put the government upon the Lord's shoulder. How would He provide? We had very little support, so we were shut up to the Lord's provision.

For many years, I traveled to a very small church in Louisville, Kentucky. People in this church prayed. There was a widowed woman who cleaned offices. When she died, she left a will that included the location of a chest where she had saved bills and spare change to be given to a missionary. How much do you think was in that chest? 3,200 dollars! He only does wondrous things!

Do you expect Him to do wonderful things? He will when you determine that the events and circumstances of life are going to be ordered by Him. Pray, "Lord, I am going to put the government upon Your shoulders. The authority for my life is in Your hands. The responsibility is Yours." Then begin each

Reflections on Faith

Day 14 AUTHORITY
(continued)

morning with, "I am all Yours today. I am trusting You to lead me step by step."

I had previously lived by faith, but this concept of authority crystallized my experience. You simply put the government upon the Lord's shoulder. The authority is His; the responsibility is His; the ordering of every detail is His.

Personal Reflections:

He Giveth More Grace

He giveth more grace when the burdens grow greater,
He sendeth more strength when the labors increase,
To added affliction He addeth His mercy,
To multiplied trials His multiplied peace.

When we have exhausted our store of endurance,
When strength has declined 'ere the day is half-done,
When we reach the end of our hoarded resources,
Our Father's full giving is only begun.

His love has no limit, His grace has no measure,
His power no boundary known unto men,
For out of His infinite riches in Jesus
He giveth and giveth and giveth again.

Annie J. Flint

Reflections on Faith

Day 15   AUTHORITY

———◆———

For unto us a child is born, unto us a son is given: and the government shall be upon his shoulder...(Isaiah 9:6).

As I considered the possibility of establishing a conference center in Greenville, South Carolina, I prayed, "Lord, give us several acres of land in a country setting within ten minutes of the city center by the first of April or we will return to Japan."

In February, we looked at a map and the first place we selected is where the EI School of Biblical Training now sits. "This would be an ideal place," I said to my wife, and she agreed. We inquired about the owner and were told, "He is a multimillionaire in his eighties who raises horses on the property. There are 40 acres and a stone house where he takes his grandchildren on weekends. There is no way he will sell this land." "Ask him," I urged, but the owner said, "No. I don't need the money, and I look forward to weekends with my grandchildren." We looked all over the city, but kept returning to this location.

"Please speak to him again." My friends said, "It is not the slightest use." We had no money, but because the authority and responsibility were the Lord's, we trusted Him to handle everything. If He was going to give us the land, He would pay for it as well. My wife and I left the matter with Him.

Reflections on Faith

Day 15 — AUTHORITY
(continued)

We were invited to the home of the pastor of the First Baptist Church. When we arrived, I was surprised to see a dear friend, Miss Martha Franks. The land owner had been visiting this pastor and said, "There is someone who wants to buy my land. I have no intention of selling, but he has been persistent. I know he was ministering in Japan. Do you know anyone who would know this man?" The pastor said, "My wife's best friend is in our kitchen. She was a missionary in China and might have heard of this man." When we ministered in Formosa, we lived in the home of Miss Martha Franks. There in that kitchen at the optimum moment was Miss Franks. When they asked whether she had ever heard of me, she said, "Oh, yes. He is a close personal friend." By the time she finished, the old gentleman was very eager to sell us the land.

We placed the government upon His shoulder. Although it seemed impossible, we purchased that land. God does wondrous things in response to faith.

Day 16   BALANCE

I am the vine, ye are the branches: He that abideth in me, and I in him, the same bringeth forth much fruit: for without me ye can do nothing (John 15:5).

The only balanced Christian is the man or woman who is habitually living by faith in the Son of God.

During the Second World War, Admiral Haulsey terrorized the Japanese with his great fleet of aircraft carriers, battleships, destroyers, and cruisers. Once he made the mistake of permitting his fleet to be overtaken by a typhoon. Three destroyers were sunk. They heeled over in the waves to a degree that allowed water to pour down their funnels.

No one understood how destroyers could sink, even in a typhoon. During an inquiry, the builders' plans were evaluated. The ships were considered perfectly balanced when they left the shipyard. In following the history of the vessels, they learned that unbalancing occurred when a variety of things were later added to the top decks. The ships sank, because they were unbalanced.

Don't add to faith. Don't act independently. Follow the Master. Faith in Him will provide the balance you need to withstand any storm or trial.

Day 17 CONSISTENCY AND STABILITY

I have set the Lord always before me: because he is at my right hand, I shall not be moved (Psalm 16:8).

The life of faith is not an on-again, off-again proposition. It's a consistent, moment-by-moment attitude and walk. Faith is not to be exercised only when you have great need.

Any soldier in basic training is taught to obey a command, and obey instantly, without question, without hesitation, and with all his heart. If he doesn't, it may cost him his life. You cannot live the Christian life apart from faith. So the psalmist tells us: *I've set the Lord always before me*. No matter what situation arises, whether desirable or undesirable, always set the Lord before you to live by faith.

Every day of your life, keep on setting Him before you; keep on trusting His faithfulness. You know that God is above your circumstances and that your circumstances are a passing phase. You know there is continuity with God.

Are you the victim of circumstances and emotion? When you know God and live by faith, you will be steady. You will be established. The consistent life of faith brings stability. Are you characterized by stability?

Reflections on Faith

Day 18 FAITH ALONE

———◆———

But without faith it is impossible to please him...(Hebrews 11:6).

It is faith alone that enables you to enter into all that the Lord has prepared for you.

Many years ago, I was ministering in Asheville, North Carolina. One cold evening, I returned to my friend's home after a meeting. When those who had driven me wanted to make certain I could enter the house, I assured them it wasn't necessary.

There was no response when I pressed and kept pressing the doorbell. I decided to go to a nearby shopping center after first looking through all the windows. As I walked against the traffic, a car rounded a curve, blinded me, and I slipped into a culvert filled with icy water. Very uncomfortable! I finally reached a motel and called the number where I thought I might find my hostess. In a rather grieved voice, I asked, "Why didn't you tell me you wouldn't be home?" I've never forgotten her answer, "Well, Mr. Carroll, I did give you a key." I put my hand in my pocket. Sure enough, there was the house key.

God has given us a key that we seldom use. While we are busy knocking at doors, ringing bells, and seeking help from other

Reflections on Faith

Day 18

FAITH ALONE
(continued)

sources, we have the key that allows us to enter into all that we need. That key is faith. Multitudes of Christians are double-minded and fearful because they have forgotten this key.

God has no substitute for faith.

Day 19   FAITH FOLLOWS

And he said unto them, Why are ye so fearful? how is it that ye have no faith? (Mark 4:40).

You can only trust the Lord to do what He's telling you to do.

The disciples in the boat thought they could sail without the Lord. Wanting to help, they took over the boat and set sail for the other side of the lake. Some of these men were fishermen who knew the sea and how to handle boats. This was something they could do, so they completely ignored the Lord. Jesus was not in control; He was not directing the action.

Invariably, when you launch your own plan, the Lord permits you to do so. "We'll take Him to the other side." Will you? A time will come when you will pay for your foolish, independent spirit. He's going to have to rescue you before it's over. Many well-meaning men have made this mistake. After Moses' great surrender to identify with Israel, he did the wrong thing with all earnestness. Any man that believes he can operate without the Lord is deluded. The disciples courted danger by delaying to awaken the Lord until they were utterly desperate. Jesus rose, graciously quieted the storm, and asked His challenging question: "Where is your faith?"

Always follow the Lord; go with Him. Faith cries, "I **must** have Your presence!"

Reflections on Faith

Day 20 FEAR VERSUS FAITH

For God hath not given us the spirit of fear; but of power, and of love, and of a sound mind (II Timothy 1:7).

One of the first weapons the enemy uses against believers is fear, fear of circumstances. Throughout the Old and New Testaments, the enemy tried to strike fear into the hearts of his intended victims. Why? If the enemy could make them afraid, they would be in deep trouble.

Mr. Bailey served in Africa and often shared stories of lions. Once, he was downwind and could watch as a lion crouched and crawled in the grass toward a water buffalo quietly drinking at the river. When he was within springing distance, the lion let out a terrible roar. As the buffalo stiffened in fear, the lion leapt, killing with one swipe of his paw to the buffalo's throat. The purpose of the roar was to immobilize the animal with fear, giving the lion an advantage over his prey.

Faith will be determined by your focus. Is your focus on circumstances or on the Sovereign Lord who is above circumstances? You are to look unto Jesus. You are to be a man of faith. You are not to be dominated by fear of circumstances.

Faith and fear cannot co-exist. You choose to be either a man of fear or a man of faith.

Day 21 MAINTAINING FAITH

...men ought always to pray, and not to faint (Luke 18:1).

Both prayer and the Word of God fuel the fire of faith. If you neglect prayer, you will faint. If you neglect the Word of God, your faith will fail. To maintain faith, it is necessary to give yourself to prayer and to meditation on the Word of God with a view to obedience.

With your act of faith, you will become a target for the wrath of the enemy. Satan will hurl everything at you, creating circumstances to disturb and distract you from expecting God to do wonderful things. At such times, faith must be fed. To keep believing, keep your eyes on the Lord by giving yourself to a life of prayer and to the study of God's Word.

God tested George Mueller's faith again and again. On one occasion, the orphans came into the large dining room for breakfast. In an act of faith, Mr. Mueller offered thanks for the meal when there was no bread to give the children. Just then, a baker, who had been unable to sleep all night, knocked at the door to leave a load of bread. There was another knock at the door. The milkman had arrived with a cartload of milk. The wheel of his horse-drawn cart had fallen off, so he was unable to make his deliveries. The orphans had bread and milk for breakfast.

Reflections on Faith

Day 21 — MAINTAINING FAITH
(continued)

This experience was rather common for Mueller. Why? He was a man of faith because he was a man of prayer and a student of the Word.

Personal Reflections:

Jesus, Master, Whose I Am

Jesus, Master, Whose I am,
Purchased Thine alone to be,
By Thy blood, O spotless Lamb,
Shed so willingly for me.
Let my heart be all Thine own,
Let me live to Thee alone.

Other lords have long held sway;
Now, Thy name alone to bear,
Thy dear voice alone obey,
Is my daily, hourly, prayer:
Whom have I in heaven but Thee?
Nothing else my joy can be.

Jesus, Master, Whom I serve,
Though so feebly and so ill,
Strengthen hand and heart and nerve
All Thy bidding to fulfill.
Open Thou my eyes to see
All the work Thou hast for me.

Jesus, Master, wilt Thou use
One who owes Thee more than all?
As Thou wilt! I would not choose;
Only let me hear Thy call.
Jesus, let me always be,
In Thy service, glad and free.

Francis Ridley Havergal

Day 22   SPIRITUAL PLACES

Blessed be the God and Father of our Lord Jesus Christ, who hath blessed us with all spiritual blessings in heavenly places in Christ (Ephesians 1:3).

There are three stratas in spiritual conflict: the earth, the powers of darkness in the heavenlies, and the heaven of heavens, which is the abode of God. In which strata do you live?

Our spiritual location is in Christ, who is seated far above in heavenly places. You look down, therefore, on earthly circumstances and powers of darkness.

The enemy tries to have you become occupied with your earthly circumstances. When this happens, instead of looking down on the powers of darkness, the powers of darkness tread upon you. If you are thinking, acting, and reacting to circumstances as a natural man, you have placed yourself under the powers of darkness. The circumstances of earth are not to dictate your actions.

Faith is only possible when circumstances do not dictate. Look down from the heavenlies, conscious that you have power and authority in Christ. You are more than a conqueror through Him who loved you. By faith, take your place in Christ, in heavenly places, above circumstances and powers, and tread down your enemies.

Reflections on Faith

Day 23 — THINK VICTORY

For whatsoever is born of God overcometh the world: and this is the victory that overcometh the world, even our faith (1 John 5:4).

Think victory! Think nothing but victory all the time! Victory is the only thing that is worthy of the Lord. As you follow Him, He leads you in victory.

If you're not thinking victory, it's because unbelief is present. You are not trusting Him to do wonderful things, so you walk around with a long face. The demeanor of the person truly trusting the Lord includes an aspect of triumph.

Victory requires faith in testing. You must keep on trusting Him despite delays. As faith is exercised, God performs His will.

Faith overcomes, so think victory!

Day 24 FAITH TRAINING

I had fainted, unless I had believed to see the goodness of the LORD in the land of the living (Psalm 27:13).

How does God train a man of faith?

God allows circumstances which are beyond your control so you will cry out to Him. He then answers, giving direction. As you follow His direction, you observe Him in action. Your commitment to what He reveals allows you to watch Him work. This is His training routine for increasing your faith.

God can not work for you if you are dominated by the horizontal, the things of earth. He only works for the man who lives above the powers of darkness, above everything taking place on this earth. While the man of faith is physically grounded, his spiritual location is in heavenly places in Christ, far above trying circumstances.

Are you in training to increase your faith? Where do you live? Are you dominated by heavenly things or by that which is seen? Are you dominated by circumstances or do you live above life's circumstances?

Reflections on Faith

Day 25   GOD'S FAITHFULNESS

And he said unto them, Why are ye so fearful? how is it that ye have no faith? (Mark 4:40).

When preparing for a series of messages, I began to read book after book in search of a definition of faith. I didn't find one. Each author talked about faith, but didn't define it. Handley Moule, after studying in Sanskrit, Latin, Hebrew, Greek, German, and English, finally prepared a simple and complete definition: "Faith is personal trust in a Person." Biblical faith is personal trust in Jesus Christ.

Faith is never faith in your faith. You do not summon up enough faith so that God will act. That's misplaced faith. The object of faith must be God Himself. This means to have faith in God's faithfulness. When you express faith, you are trusting God's faithfulness.

When Wesley was crossing the Atlantic on his way to the United States, his vessel encountered a terrible storm. Many feared the ship would sink. People were screaming, and Wesley was terrified. There was a small group of Moravian missionaries aboard who were perfectly calm. Even the children were quiet. The difference between his reaction to possible death and the reaction of the Moravians spoke to Wesley.

Faith anchors you in life's storms; it enables you to stand, to remain immovable.

Day 26 — CIRCUMSTANCES

But they that wait upon the LORD shall renew their strength; they shall mount up with wings as eagles; they shall run, and not be weary; and they shall walk, and not faint (Isaiah 40:31).

God wants to teach you to fly. He wants you to soar as a man of faith, living above your circumstances, living above conditions which would terrify those not living by faith. Faith enables you to effortlessly soar above life's difficulties.

Consider the eagle. He hardly flaps his wings, yet he flies with fantastic speed. He knows how to take advantage of air currents. That's the difference between the eagle and the person being pushed by circumstances. When the currents of circumstances sweep against you, they can destroy you. For the man of faith, the same currents will lift him into the heights, higher and nearer to his Lord. He is living by faith, not by sight, not by feelings. His life is not dictated by circumstances. His eyes are on the Lord.

How do you react in the difficult place?

Reflections on Faith

Day 27   FAITH REWARDED

I press toward the mark for the prize of the high calling of God in Christ Jesus (Philippians 3:14).

The Apostle Paul, nearing the end of his race, is still pressing forward; he's still giving all he has, all the time. There is a sense of striving toward a goal in his words.

God rewards those who diligently seek Him. This is why God rewarded Paul, and this is why God will reward you or me if we determine to know Him.

This doesn't mean seeking God's blessings or His favor. We seek God Himself, His Person. He rewards those with the intensity of purpose to press forward to know Him. He rewards those who diligently seek Him.

Day 28 — SATISFACTION

For to me to live is Christ...(Philippians 1:21).

Life is Christ. What does this mean? Christ has become your satisfaction.

Not until Christ is your life, your satisfaction, will you have protection against the devil's attempts to displace Him with other things. If distracted, you will suddenly find yourself living for this, this, and this. When you turn to other sources, you are seeking the wrong experience. No human experience on earth can satisfy the depths of your human need. That is not possible; God will not permit that to happen. Do you seek satisfaction apart from God?

Many of your problems may arise from anticipations. You have a reaction to unrealized expectations. When not realized, you seek satisfaction from sources other than God. The Lord wants to divorce you from operating in this way. He wants to set you free with perfect freedom, so that you may live for others while experiencing satisfaction in Him.

You must ask yourself, "Is Jesus Christ my satisfaction, my life, my all?" As Augustine well said, "He has made us for Himself, and we can never rest until we rest in Him."

Personal Reflections:

We Rest on Thee

We rest on Thee, our Shield and our Defender;
We go not forth alone against the foe.
Strong in Thy strength, safe in Thy keeping tender,
We rest on Thee, and in Thy Name we go.

Yea, in Thy Name, O Captain of salvation!
In Thy dear Name, all other names above;
Jesus our Righteousness, our sure Foundation,
Our Prince of glory and our King of love.

We go in faith, our own great weakness feeling,
And needing more each day Thy grace to know -
Yet from our hearts a song of triumph pealing:
We rest on Thee, and in Thy Name we go.

We rest on Thee, our Shield and our Defender.
Thine is the battle - Thine shall be the praise!
When passing through the gates of pearly splendor,
Victors, we rest with Thee, through endless days.

         E.G. Cherry

Day 29   SUFFICIENCY

I can do all things through Christ which strengtheneth me (Philippians 4:13).

The apostle Paul said, *I can do all things through Christ which strengtheneth me*. Paul is saying, "There is nothing I cannot do because I am Christ's and, therefore, through Christ, I can do all things." Here is a man who found his sufficiency in the indwelling Christ.

You can do all things through Christ who strengthens you. A free translation would be, "Who pours the power into you when you need it." That is beautiful!

Is Christ your sufficiency?

Day 30   SECURITY

But my God shall supply all your need according to his riches in glory by Christ Jesus (Philippians 4:19).

...I will be with thee: I will not fail thee, nor forsake thee (Joshua 1:5).

God must become your security. If He isn't your security, you will look to other sources such as possessions or assets or friends. There is no genuine security to be found in these.

God said to Joshua, "I will not fail you; I will not forsake you. I will be with you wherever you go." Joshua's security was found in a Person, God Himself.

Do you believe, do you know, that God will richly supply all your needs in Jesus Christ? I mean *ALL* your needs. This verse speaks of much more than bread and butter. When Scripture speaks of all your needs, it includes the deep emotional needs of your heart.

God supplies everything you need according to His riches in Christ Jesus. Security flows from the assurance that a sovereign God is present and able to supply any need you might have through Jesus Christ. That's enough for all of life.

Is your security found in Christ?

Reflections on Faith

Day 31 FAITH'S HAND

...let him come unto me, and drink (John 7:37).

Jesus' invitation was very simple: *come...and drink*. There's no substitute for the outstretched hand of faith. You respond by taking. The hand of faith must take or lay hold of what is offered. Whenever the will of God is revealed, there must be the response of faith.

The woman whose sons were about to be taken to be bondsmen had nothing left in her house. Everything was gone, every stick of furniture, rugs, everything. Then she cried to the prophet. His words demanded faith, a great deal of faith. She was to get water jars, any kind of jar: ornate, plain, gold, silver, clay. She was to pour the oil into the vessels and she would be able to pay her debt, redeem her sons, and live. She must do what she was told to do. That's all we have to do at any time.

Remember the widow who heard Elijah's instruction and responded by making a cake for him with her last oil and flour. When told to do a very difficult thing from a human viewpoint, she responded in faith, simply doing what she was told to do. This widow didn't allow unbelief to cause her to question the prophet's words.

You must respond to God's revealed will with the outstretched hand of faith.

Faith moves and works in the dark, in the unknown, and in the unseen, but never without a sense of direction.

- Handley Moule

Prayer Journal

Prayer

Month 2

Every work of God can be traced

to a kneeling figure.

— D. L. Moody

Jesus, the Name High Over All

Jesus, the name to sinners dear,
The name to sinners given;
It scatters all their guilty fear,
It turns their hell to heaven.

Jesus the prisoner's fetters breaks,
And bruises Satan's head;
Power into strengthless souls He speaks,
And life into the dead.

Oh, that the world might taste and see
The riches of His grace!
The arms of love that compass me
Would all mankind embrace.

Charles Wesley

Day 1   PRAY FIRST

But we will give ourselves continually to prayer, and to the ministry of the word (Acts 6:4).

Handley Moule said, "We should pray first." When confronted with a situation, we are apt to think, "What is the answer?" Next we pick up the telephone and ask someone for their comments. By Sunday morning, we may go to the pastor to learn his thoughts on the matter. You may become utterly confused after seeking the advice of those you trust. We should not think first. No! Pray first.

In the early church, the apostles gave themselves first to prayer and then to the preaching of the Word, despite problems which arose that could have diverted them from this emphasis.

In the great conflict of life, the person who makes the most mistakes loses. God never makes mistakes. He alone has the answers you need, so go to the Lord first. Pray first!

Day 2   CYCLE OF PRAYER

*Likewise the Spirit also helpeth our infirmities:
for we know not what we should pray...* (Romans 8:26).

These steps constitute the cycle of prayer:

> the will of God, the Father,
> known by the Spirit,
> revealed to the believer,
> who prays in Jesus' name, our only access.

A. W. Pink said, "Man can no more pray without the Holy Ghost than he can create a world." This is a true statement, although perhaps difficult to accept. We understand that no one can create a world, not even a blade of grass; but Pink assures us we cannot pray without the Holy Spirit. If this is true, we are completely dependent on the Holy Spirit in prayer.

Likewise the Spirit also helpeth our infirmities: for we know not what we should pray for as we ought.... The testimony of God's Word is that we do not know what to pray. Only the Spirit knows: *but the Spirit itself maketh intercession for us with groanings which cannot be uttered. And he that searcheth the heart knoweth what is the mind of the Spirit, because he* [that is the Spirit] *maketh intercession for the saints according to the will of God* (Romans 8:26-27).

Reflections on Prayer

Day 3   CYCLE OF PRAYER

And this is the confidence that we have in him, that if we ask anything according to his will, he heareth us: And if we know that he hear us, whatsoever we ask, we know that we have the petitions that we desired of him (I John 5:14-15).

Prevailing prayer is aligned with God's will, and only the Spirit knows His will.

A man praying in the Spirit for five minutes can achieve more than the man praying for a year without the Spirit.

Believers are a kingdom of priests and intercessors. As we ask according to God's will, we have assurance: *And this is the confidence that we have in him, that if we ask anything according to his will, he heareth us: And if we know that he hear us, whatsoever we ask, we know that we have the petitions that we desired of him.* This wonderful promise gives us confidence that our petitions will be granted when aligned with God's will.

Prayer is not an exercise of "maybe" or "perhaps." If we pray according to God's will, we have the assurance of answers. We know we have the petitions we desire as we wait for the answers.

Reflections on Prayer

Day 4   CYCLE OF PRAYER

...My grace is sufficient for thee: for my strength is made perfect in weakness...(2 Corinthians 12:9).

Our helplessness in intercession qualifies us for dependence on the Spirit of God, for God's strength is made perfect in our weakness. For the power of Christ to rest upon us, we must be conscious of our helplessness.

Prayer can not be "packaged" intercession. The Spirit of God is sovereign, always doing new things. Because we do not know what to pray, we must depend on the Spirit each and every time we intercede.

Faith and fear cannot coexist. Once you doubt that the indwelling Spirit of God will guide your prayer, His empowering work ceases. The Spirit is within us to reveal God's will; therefore, surrender and faith is necessary if we are to pray in the Spirit.

We must be babes in our faith, in our dependence, in our openness and receptivity. We must be babes who are conscious of our need in prayer. God created us to receive. We must receive a knowledge of God's will in order to pray. As we depend, trust, and receive, we truly intercede.

Day 5   CYCLE OF PRAYER

And all things, whatsoever ye shall ask in prayer, believing, ye shall receive (Matthew 21:22).

The believer is the only point in the cycle of prayer where a breakdown may occur.

We fellowship with God as we cooperate in His earthly work through the ministry of intercession. For the believer, prayer is a far greater obligation than our obligation to witness or teach. Being prepared to intercede in the Spirit is our supreme duty.

Only God can do the work of God. He uses instruments, but He does the work, and Scripture makes it clear that He moves when men pray. John Wesley once made a rather startling statement that not everyone agrees is correct. He said, "God does nothing but in answer to prayer."

Believers can speak with people thousands of times about Christ's death for their sins and receive only blank stares in response. When the Holy Spirit shines just a little ray of light into their darkened hearts, they see truth. Blindness reigns until God moves.

I wrestled with this reality in my early evangelistic campaigns. In one small country town, the Spirit of God would move and people would be wonderfully saved. In another little town,

Day 5 — CYCLE OF PRAYER
(continued)

the atmosphere would be dead. The same preaching, the same approach, bore very different results. I asked the Lord, "Why?" As I studied Scripture, the difference became clear. The Spirit moves when men pray. It is prayer in the Spirit that makes the difference. Where there is a moving of the Spirit, there is lively intercession. Where there is no intercession, there is no moving of the Spirit.

Reflections on Prayer

Day 6   IMPRESSIONS

I will extol thee, O Lord, for thou hast lifted me up, and hast not made my foes to rejoice over me (Psalm 30:1).

Faint impressions often come as you walk in the Spirit in surrender and faith. Never ignore them. When the Spirit of God speaks, we must listen and retain the impressions.

In a time of great need, the Spirit may use dramatic means to urge you to pray. Perhaps He will vividly bring a person in crisis to your mind. You might wonder, "Why am I thinking of this person?"

Mr. Bailey did pioneer work in Africa. Once he walked into a bathhouse and was confronted by a coiled, spitting cobra. This type of cobra blinds the victim by spraying poison into their eyes. Mr. Bailey froze, believing himself to be a dead man, expecting to feel the poison at any moment. As he waited, the cobra uncharacteristically backed into a corner to glare at him. He wondered, "Why did the snake back away?"

Years later, while on furlough, Mr. Bailey heard the story of a young mother. As she was nursing her baby on the veranda, she suddenly saw Mr. Bailey as clearly as if he had been photographed. She saw fear on his face, began to pray, and was covered with sweat when she concluded her prayer. Mr. Bailey asked the young woman about the date and time of this event

Day 6 — IMPRESSIONS
(continued)

and realized that it corresponded with the time he faced the cobra. The Spirit of God had called upon the young mother to pray because she was available and ready.

Take time to be still and to pray. Unless it is an extreme emergency, the Spirit of God doesn't shout. Don't ignore His voice of gentle stillness.

Day 7 PRAYER PARTNER

...if two of you shall agree on earth as touching any thing that they shall ask, it shall be done for them of my Father which is in heaven (Matthew 18:19).

A prayer partner is a great advantage in detecting the will of God. Praying with a partner with whom you have oneness of spirit results in greater power. I once had such a partner who kept a journal of our petitions and showed me the long list of answered prayers. He said, "Do you realize that every time we were conscious of praying in the Spirit and claimed the answer from God, our prayer was answered?"

How would you know if you are praying in the Spirit with your prayer partner? The Spirit gives the same impression to both people. It is not a matter of agreeing between you that God will do something. When the burden on one heart answers the burden upon the other person's heart, the two are symphonizing in the Spirit. When prayer is under the Spirit's control, God grants the petitions.

Don't come to prayer with a hope-so attitude. Come with confidence based on Matthew 18:19: *...if two of you shall agree on earth as touching any thing that they shall ask, it shall be done for them of my Father which is in heaven.*

Personal Reflections:

*Learn to move men through
God by prayer alone.*
— Hudson Taylor

Reflections on Prayer

Day 8   PREVAILING IN PRAYER

Who shall ascend into the hill of the Lord? or who shall stand in His holy place? (Psalm 24:3).

Prayer is actually the highest art of which man is capable; it is effective communion with one's Maker.

In Psalm 24, we have a moral description of the man God blesses when he comes to pray. We must, however, differentiate between gaining access to God and prevailing with Him. We have access at any time through Christ's blood and victory; however, there are moral conditions necessary to prevail in prayer.

Verse 3 goes to the very heart of the matter: *Who shall ascend into the hill of the Lord? or who shall stand in His holy place?* Notice that the Scripture says we stand in His *holy* place. The emphasis here is on holiness.

The Psalmist gives three conditions for prevailing prayer:

- *He that hath clean hands* – an abstinence from evil actions.

- *And a pure heart* – an abstinence from evil thoughts; pure motives.

Day 8   PREVAILING IN PRAYER
(continued)

- *Who hath not lifted up his soul unto vanity* – remembering that you are bound to God and must seek his glory alone.

Satan fears the intercessor because prayer brings God into action. To avoid defeat, he does everything he can to turn you from living by these moral requirements. The Lord must deliver us from the devil's snares if we are to experience a life of prevailing prayer.

Reflections on Prayer

Day 9 PREVAILING IN PRAYER

———◆———

Wash you, make you clean; put away the evil of your doings from before mine eyes; cease to do evil; Learn to do well... (Isaiah 1:16-17).

What is the first instruction? *Wash you, make you clean.* Your part is to submit to cleansing. When the Spirit of God speaks, do not argue or delay. Sometimes you delay for days, weeks, or even months. Perhaps when the Spirit of God first spoke, you were conscious of your need, but with your delay, your conscience eventually became seared.

I used to suffer from chronic rhinitis. In hay fever season, my nostrils would be distended, completely blocked, and my eyes would almost close. A friend sent me to the ear, nose, and throat specialist used by the royal family. This physician examined me very closely and cauterized some spots on my membrane. As he touched these spots with a red-hot needle, he warned me, "You must not have this done very often. Every time I touch your membrane, I am searing it. If I continue touching your tissue with this needle, you will lose all sensitivity."

Your conscience is far more sensitive. When you sin, your reaction is like a red-hot needle touching your conscience. This is the Spirit of God saying, "This is wrong." When you fail to respond and continue repeating the sin, the needle keeps touching until your conscience becomes insensitive and ceases to respond. Cleansing is a prerequisite of prevailing prayer.

Day 10 PREVAILING PRAYER

Wash you, make you clean; put away the evil of your doings from before mine eyes; cease to do evil; Learn to do well...(Isaiah 1:16-17).

I remember reading about a triggerman with Murder, Incorporated. Give him 1,000 dollars; name the victim; and he would commit the murder. After completing his first assignment, he was actually sick and could not eat or sleep for days. With the next few murders, he felt very little. After a dozen jobs, he felt nothing and returned home to sleep quite soundly. His conscience had become seared. He no longer reacted to taking a life.

Come now, and let us reason together, saith the Lord: though your sins be as scarlet, they shall be as white as snow; though they be red like crimson, they shall be as wool (Isaiah 1:18).

It is a wonderful thing that the conscience can be renewed, but you must be willing to confess and repent of your sin. The beautiful scarlet cloth worn by the nobility of Isaiah's day had been dipped into the vat of dye, dried, and immersed again until the threads were so saturated that the color could not be removed. With this picture, the Lord is saying, "Though you have plunged yourself again and again into sin until you are saturated with it, you can be as white as snow." What a picture of the power of Christ's blood for cleansing!

Reflections on Prayer

Day 11   CLEAN HANDS

Wash you, make you clean; put away the evil of your doings from before mine eyes; cease to do evil...(Isaiah 1:16).

Clean hands are indicative of a holy character and are the first condition for prayer. The Psalmist would stand before God with his arms outstretched and his palms lifted to visibly represent a holy character and clean hands. You must come to prayer with the same testimony.

John Stott made a striking statement: "There is no happiness without holiness." Do not be indifferent to sin. Sin grieves the Spirit of God, and when the Spirit is grieved, you cannot prevail in prayer. You are rendered helpless, for the Spirit alone knows the will of God.

You walk with a holy God. In yourself, you are unholy, but in Christ, you are holy. You contribute nothing to this holiness. Appropriating Christ's holiness as your own is God's provision. You begin as perfect in Christ and aim at perfection in your experience. It is a paradox. You are sanctified in Christ, but you are also *being* sanctified. You are holy, and you are also to become holy. Knowing that you are apt to stray should not destroy your confidence. Concentrate on your Savior, not your sinfulness. You enter God's presence with Christ's holy character to pray and to prevail in prayer.

Day 12   CONFESSION

Search me, O God, and know my heart; try me, and know my thoughts: And see if there be any wicked way in me...
(Psalm 139:23-24).

The unclean must enter God's presence through confession and repentance. This is always a fundamental condition for prevailing prayer.

Do not be taken up with sin nor occupied with yourself, for neither will inspire. In your daily walk, your great concern should be to remain sensitive to the Spirit of God. You cannot be occupied with sin and the Spirit at the same time. Remember the Psalmist did not look within his heart and ask, "What is wrong with me?" He did not engage in introspection. Let the Spirit of God inspect you. Quietly wait upon the Lord so He might reveal your sin. Without such times, we are apt to develop habitual sins.

When I was a small boy, I detested and feared the dentist. I would cry because I knew he would use that painful probe. Later, I understood that the dentist was helping me. Early discovery of a cavity meant I would endure less pain. The Lord also desires to help you. Be willing to undergo His necessary probing so that you might confess, repent, and be cleansed.

Reflections on Prayer

Day 13   CONFESSION

———————◆———————

If we confess our sins, he is faithful and just to forgive us our sins, and to cleanse us from all unrighteousness (1 John 1:9).

Confession and repentance should take no more than 30 seconds. It is the blood of Jesus that saves you, not seasons of moaning and groaning. This is a lesson not easily learned by a young Christian. You fall short of your ideal and, if you are not careful, you fall into a pit. I used to go into the blackest of pits for weeks at a time. "Why did I sin? How could I fail again?" Then the Lord taught me that 30 seconds is all it takes. At some point in time, you must get out of the pit and move on, so you might as well do it now.

Bertha Smith, a missionary to China, presented the truth of confession to one girl in a unique way. "Stop trying to take up your cross. How can you while you are dirty and unclean? Do you think you can follow Him with a dirty heart? Put your sins on the cross and jump on that cross yourself." You might question the accuracy of her theology, but do you get her point? Put your filthiness on the cross and jump on yourself, then you can walk, as Bertha expressed it, with your sins "confessed-and-up-to-date."

Day 14 — REPENT

Wash you, make you clean; put away the evil of your doings from before mine eyes; cease to do evil; Learn to do well...though your sins be as scarlet, they shall be white as snow...If ye be willing and obedient, ye shall eat the good of the land (Isaiah 1:16-19).

Not only must there be confession of sin but also repentance. We turn from evil to return with a willing and obedient heart to what God requires. Do you have a willing heart? Are you wholehearted when it comes to dealing with sin? You must immediately deal with whatever God reveals is wrong.

"Did you get it all?" is the first question to ask your doctor after cancer surgery. Cancer threatens your life. You need all those cancer cells removed. Sin is even more vicious than cancer. It hinders your prayer life. You must have a willing heart expressed through obedience for sin to be removed. You must be finished with your sin. Never be halfhearted or lukewarm with the Lord.

Wholeheartedness brings a manifestation of God's power in prayer. If we are willing and obedient, there will be blessing: *...ye shall eat the good of the land.*

Personal Reflections:

Have Thine Own Way, Lord

Have Thine own way, Lord,
Have Thine own way;
Thou art the Potter - I am the clay.
Mold me and make me after Thy will,
While I am waiting, yielded and still.

Have Thine own way, Lord,
Have Thine own way;
Search me and try me, Master, today.
Whiter than snow, Lord, wash me just now,
As in Thy presence humbly I bow.

Have Thine own way, Lord,
Have Thine own way;
Wounded and weary, help me, I pray.
Power, all power, surely is Thine,
Touch me and heal me, Savior divine.

Have Thine own way, Lord,
Have Thine own way;
Hold o'er my being absolute sway.
Fill with Thy Spirit 'til all shall see
Christ only, always, living in me.

A. A. Pollard

Reflections on Prayer

Day 15   A PURE HEART

Who shall ascend into the hill of the Lord? or who shall stand in His holy place? He that hath clean hands, and a pure heart...
(Psalm 24:3-4).

Draw nigh to God, and He will draw nigh to you. Cleanse your hands, ye sinners; and purify your hearts, ye double minded
(James 4:8).

James gives us strong, forthright words concerning how to draw near to God. He says to first *cleanse your hands,* and then to *purify your hearts.* A pure heart is a heart with right motives, right feelings, and right aims. This does not mean a sinless heart.

What is the right motive in prayer? Are you seeking answers to your prayers for your sake? A pure heart desires that God will be glorified. This is the ultimate motive needed for prevailing intercession.

Consider Adoniram Judson, the great missionary to Burma. The King of Burma said, "We care nothing for his message. We care nothing for his God. We care nothing for his Bible, but his scars are irresistible." When the missionary and his message are rejected, only a desire for the glory of God will sustain him.

Judson's suffering testified to the Burmese of his desire for the glory of God.

Day 15   A PURE HEART
(continued)

Judson's first wife died; his children died; his second wife died. He kept going. He was living for the glory of God. One writer said, "Judson founded the church in Burma in granite." He did so because he had a pure heart.

The glory of God is a powerful motive. Nothing else can keep you steady when the path is hard. When you say, "I am going to glorify God by my submission and obedience and leave the rest with Him," you are expressing a pure heart.

Reflections on Prayer

Day 16 A PURE HEART

Ye lust, and have not: ye kill, and desire to have, and cannot obtain: ye fight and war, yet ye have not, because ye ask not. Ye ask, and receive not, because ye ask amiss, that ye may consume it upon your lusts (James 4:2-3).

James is saying, "Because your motives are wrong, you do not receive." Because their hearts were dissatisfied, they did not pray. When they did pray, because their motives were to satisfy their lusts, they did not receive answers to their prayers.

A pure heart is single-minded: possessing a single objective or aim and operating from a single motive. Do you have a single aim? Married or unmarried, preacher or street sweeper, missionary or housewife, do you live for the glory of God?

To prevail in prayer, you must have a pure heart that ultimately desires the glory of God.

Day 17   VANITY

Who shall ascend into the hill of the Lord? or who shall stand in His holy place? He that hath clean hands, and a pure heart; who hath not lifted up his soul unto vanity...(Psalm 24:3-4).

The man with clean hands and a pure heart is also a man who is neither deflected nor dominated by temporal desires. This man is characterized by a longing to know and do God's will. He is not taken up with those things that could even be deemed permissible.

This condition for prevailing prayer means you are content with God's will. Whether He gives you the ministry you desire or one you would never choose, you are His servant on this earth. This man will thank God with equal heartiness if life unfolds as he hopes or proves very difficult.

Struggling to accept God's will often leads to becoming occupied with "if only." Be content with the Lord's plan rather than grasping something for yourself. You must let everything go before you can embrace what God has for you. *Therefore glorify God in your body, and in your spirit, which are God's* (I Corinthians 6:20). The man whose soul is free of vanity is the man who daily remembers the vows by which he is bound to God. He knows that he does not belong to himself; therefore, he does not live for self-satisfaction. He is content with God's will.

Reflections on Prayer

Day 18   VANITY

Who shall ascend into the hill of the Lord? or who shall stand in His holy place? He that hath clean hands, and a pure heart; who hath not lifted up his soul unto vanity...(Psalm 24:3-4).

If you clutch what belongs to God, you lift up your soul unto vanity. You need an open hand to receive what God has for your life. You must release the beloved thing to accept His will.

Once a mother took her little boy to hear the famous evangelist, Gypsy Smith. After the meeting, they waited in line so her son might have the privilege of shaking Gypsy's hand. When the moment arrived, the proud mother said to her child, "Shake hands with Gypsy."

The little boy looked at his mother and said, "I won't."

Shattered and confused by his refusal, she repeated, "Shake hands with Gypsy."

Again he said, "No."

When he continued to refuse, she led him away, paddled him hard, then returned to the line. Once again face-to-face with the evangelist, the mother insisted, "Shake hands with Gypsy."

"I won't," came the reply.

Day 18 — VANITY
(continued)

The mother led her son away and paddled him again.

For the third time, they approached Gypsy. This time, when he was told to shake hands, the little fellow, with tears rolling down his cheeks, opened his hand to obey. In his hand was a great big English penny, which should have been placed in the collection plate.

He had kept that which belonged to God, so he could not shake hands. His mother watched as her son transferred the penny to his other palm in order to accept Gypsy's hand.

Preoccupation with temporal things hinders prevailing prayer. You need an open hand when you pray.

You need a life that is content with the will of God.

Reflections on Prayer

Day 19 ACCOMPANIMENTS TO PRAYER

O thou that hearest prayer, unto thee shall all flesh come.
(Psalm 65:2).

The New Testament reveals eight accompaniments to prayer. These are all attitudes to be found in the heart of the one who truly seeks God.

A man or woman of God will pray,
> trusting His **faithfulness** to fulfill His promises,
> **freely** pouring out his heart,
> **watching** expectantly,
> **obeying** from a surrendered will,
> **fasting** to detach himself from the world,
> **forgiving** because he has been forgiven,
> with **thanksgiving**, because he knows he has the requests which were offered,
> while **joyously** walking in the Spirit.

Because prayer is so fundamental for fruitfulness, it is important to understand the relationship of these attitudes to prayer.

Day 20 ACCOMPANIMENTS: Faith

Therefore I say unto you, What things soever ye desire, when ye pray, believe that ye receive them, and ye shall have them
(Mark 11:24).

Faith is both a requirement for prayer and a result of prayer; therefore, the man of prayer is *always* a man of faith. Believe God as you pray. When you finish, thank God that He has heard and rise from your knees to maintain an attitude of faith by expecting God to answer.

Faith must have an object and a warrant. The object of faith determines the quality and power of prayer. Our warrant is Scripture. God reveals His faithfulness through fulfilling all the promises found in His Word. He then looks for faith which is based upon His faithfulness to keep His promises.

The Object: When the Bible speaks about faith, it is invariably speaking about personal trust in a Person. *He that cometh to God must believe that He is, and that He is a rewarder of them that diligently seek Him* (Hebrews 11:6). You must ultimately trust God rather than His promises. You are dealing with some*one* rather than some*thing*. Be taken up with the God who has made the promises.

Faith is based upon God's faithfulness, not your wobbly faith. God's faithfulness is always the same, and your

Day 20   ACCOMPANIMENTS: Faith
(continued)

faith is anchored by His faithfulness to honor His Word. It does not matter how difficult the situation, faith anticipates proof of God's faithfulness.

The Warrant: Your prayer is based on His Word. There are times when you plead on the basis of a single promise. Your faith accepts His Word, and you pray with confidence that He hears and will answer. Study God's promises and learn to claim them before His throne. When you pray, hold God to His Word.

Reflections on Prayer

Day 21 ACCOMPANIMENTS: Freedom

And this is the confidence that we have in Him, that, if we ask any thing according to His will, He heareth us: And if we know that he hear us, whatsoever we ask, we know that we have the petitions that we desired of Him (1 John 5:14-15).

A spirit of freedom must accompany prayer. By this I mean confidence, freedom of speech, unreserved conversation as between those who fully trust each other.

In I John, we find this theme of confidence, boldness, and unreserved speech that tells God everything. In the presence of a friend you trust, you pour out your heart, knowing he will listen and keep your confidence, assured of his love and acceptance. You do not have to prove anything to this friend. The Lord has a listening ear. His eyes are upon the righteous and His ears are open to their cry. He is the friend who sticks closer than a brother. You can pour out your heart before Him in perfect freedom because He loves you.

Prayer is not a performance. In its essence, prayer is a pouring out of your heart to God. Worship, intercession, and petitions spill out before your Refuge. You share the burdens, desires, and longings of your heart with Him. He is the Friend of friends who will listen and answer.

The next time you pray, come with a spirit of confidence; come with perfect freedom; come with an attitude of faith to tell Him everything. Have no fear about the words you will speak. Even

Day 21 ACCOMPANIMENTS: Freedom
(continued)

if you fumble your words, God hears your prayer before you even open your mouth. It is the cry of your heart that counts.

With perfect freedom, speak to the One you trust.

Personal Reflections:

Prayer

*I would rather teach one man to pray
than ten to preach.*

- John Henry Jowett

Day 22 ACCOMPANIMENTS: Watching

Praying always with all prayer and supplication in the Spirit, and watching thereunto with all perseverance (Ephesians 6:18).

Prayer must be accompanied by watching. The meaning of "watch" is expectation, so in prayer, you watch with expectation. One scholar points out that we never find an object to the word "watch" throughout the New Testament. We are never told what to watch. Scripture does not say to watch your enemies or Satan or yourself. You are to look unto Jesus, not within or around. This is inspiring. The Psalmist says: *...in the morning will I direct my prayer unto thee, and will look up* (Psalm 5:3).

Often people rise from their knees wondering what the enemy is going to do next. Looking for the enemy leads to fear. Pray, look unto Jesus, and expectantly watch for His answer.

Neither does the Bible tell us to watch our sins. Once a famous preacher came to Japan to minister to missionaries. He used the phrase: "hang out your dirty washing on the line." He hoped for a breakthrough in confession of sin. There is not much inspiration in sticking your nose in the garbage can. Why not live in the presence of God rather than sin or yourself?

Be occupied with the Lord who will lead you into accomplishing His purpose. Look unto Jesus.

Reflections on Prayer

Day 23   ACCOMPANIMENTS: Obedience

And whatsoever we ask, we receive of him, because we keep his commandments, and do those things that are pleasing in his sight
(1 John 3:22).

Prayer must be accompanied by obedience, which proves your love for the Lord. We often have a superficial attitude toward sin, not fearing or hating it; yet, our Lord loved righteousness and hated iniquity. Do those things that please God, keeping the keel of your ship of life far away from the sandbar of sin. Why do we tempt the Lord by sailing as close to the rocks as possible?

We need to have a horror of sin. With a coiled rattlesnake, you would not reason, "How far can this rattlesnake strike? I judge his striking range to be four feet; so, I will stand four feet and one inch away so he will just miss me." If you would never approach a rattlesnake in this manner, why do you approach sin in this way? Sin is far more deadly than the snake because it can take a man to hell or grieve the Holy Spirit. Stay clear of sin. Flee from that which you know is displeasing to the Lord.

If I regard iniquity in my heart, the Lord will not hear me (Psalm 66:18). This is a very solemn warning. If you continue in (or coddle) iniquity, the Lord will not hear. The area where you consistently fall is the area you have not fully surrendered to the Lord. The enemy will attack the weakest portion of your

Day 23 ACCOMPANIMENTS: Obedience
(continued)

line of defense. Living to please God demands that you stop what you should not be doing and stop now. You can quit any sin at any time when you are desperate enough to accept the Lord's deliverance.

You must surrender your will to God resolutely and definitely in any area that displeases Him. As soon as sin raises its ugly head, hit it hard and it will go. Then you will walk in obedience and find God wonderfully answering your prayers.

Reflections on Prayer

Day 24 ACCOMPANIMENT: Fasting

And I set my face unto the Lord God, to seek by prayer and supplications, with fasting...(Daniel 9:3).

Prayer may also be accompanied by fasting. Fasting does not necessarily mean abstinence from food. It really refers to detachment. Fasting is detachment from the things of time and sense in order to be attached to the things of God. For three weeks, Daniel did not touch any pleasant food. In other words, he detached himself from his usual way of life in order that there might be an attachment to the spiritual world. This can mean food, of course, but it can also mean recreation, friendships, or even the most intimate experience in marriage.

It is very important that even the most precious things you have in life should not master or enslave you. You must maintain mastery over them. Your body can enslave you very quickly. Paul said, "I buffet my body and bring it into subjection." Another translation says, "I beat my body black and blue and drag it around as a slave."

General Montgomery was a fantastic disciplinarian. He could say to his body, "Sleep!" and it slept. During the Battle of Ale, with a thousand guns roaring, Monty said, "Well, I am going to bed. They will not need me for at least eight hours." That was discipline!

Day 24 ACCOMPANIMENT: Fasting
(continued)

If ever a man was disciplined, it was Wesley. One volume after another of his diaries, along with his letters, were all written by hand. Traveling on horseback, he preached a thousand times a year in his eighties. It is amazing what you can accomplish if only you will give yourself to the Lord and determine that you are going to live for Him.

Fasting is detachment from earthly pursuits to spend time focusing on the things of God.

Day 25 ACCOMPANIMENTS: Forgiveness

And when ye stand praying, forgive, if ye have ought against any: that your Father also which is in heaven may forgive you your trespasses. But if you do not forgive, neither will your Father which is in heaven forgive your trespasses (Mark 11:25-26).

Prayer must be accompanied by forgiveness. Whenever you come to pray, you must not have an unforgiving spirit towards any person on the face of the earth.

In my ministry to missionaries, I found bitterness to be their most common sin. It would begin with a critical attitude, which would become an unforgiving spirit, which developed into bitterness. Forgive immediately. Never let a critical thought take root in your heart. Crush the serpent in the egg before it hatches. If you wait, the critical attitude grows larger and becomes harder to handle. Forgiveness saves you from bitterness which invariably follows an unforgiving attitude.

A root of bitterness short-circuits your prayer life. Regardless of childhood scars, you must forgive. You must be able to say, "I do not have a settled, negative attitude toward anyone on the face of the earth." If you bear a grudge or resentment or anger or malice in your heart, there is absolutely no possibility for answered prayer. The Word of God is clear that I must maintain a forgiving spirit to prevail in prayer.

Day 26 ACCOMPANIMENT: Thanksgiving

Be careful for nothing; but in every thing by prayer and application with thanksgiving let your requests be made known unto God (Philippians 4:6).

Prayer must be accompanied by thanksgiving. We seldom find prayer mentioned without thanksgiving, especially in the epistles of Paul. Why is this? It has been suggested that thanksgiving is appropriation. Petition or supplication is asking. *Ye have not because ye ask not* (James 4:2). *Ask, and it shall be given you* (Matthew 7:7). Once you have asked, you give thanks for the answer you will receive. The Scripture says that you have what you desired, so give thanks. *And this is the confidence that we have in him, that, if we ask any thing according to his will, he heareth us, And if we know that he hear us, whatsoever we ask, we know that we have the petitions that we desired of him* (1 John 5:14-15).

The question comes, "Do I pray for this again?" Pray as the Spirit prompts you. You are dealing with God, who dwells outside time. He hears and answers you the first time you pray, and so you give thanks; but if the Spirit of God continues to burden you, pour out your heart before Him. When you are no longer burdened, you cease to pray. Give thanks and it is finished.

We give thanks that the Lord has heard us. We give thanks that He is faithful to His Word. We give thanks that He has answered. In giving thanks, we are coming back to the element of faith.

Reflections on Prayer

Day 27 ACCOMPANIMENTS: Joy

Always in every prayer of mine for you all making request with joy
(Philippians 1:4).

Prayer must be accompanied by joy. Philippians 4 and Romans 12:12 teach us that joy comes first. The joyous man does not find it difficult to pray with thanksgiving. Do you make your requests with joy?

One man well versed in matters of the deeper Christian life said, "In some respects, this [joy] is the deepest and most inclusive element [of prayer]." Does that surprise you?

How do you become joyous? By looking unto Jesus? By walking in the Spirit? Yes, but to walk in the Spirit you must be holy unto the Lord. There is no joy without holiness. Holiness simply means living the way you ought to live because of what Jesus has done for you. It means offering yourself as a living sacrifice every day, which is your reasonable service. There is nothing mysterious about holiness.

"But am I not already holy in Christ?" You must become in experience what you are positionally. Thank God that we are holy in Christ. If this were not true, we could not come into God's presence. But it is also our privilege and potential to live a holy life for Jesus' sake. A life of holiness is basically going to determine whether or not we will pray with joy in the Spirit.

Day 28   THE INTERCESSOR

And I sought for a man among them, that should make up the hedge, and stand in the gap before me for the land, that I should not destroy it...(Ezekiel 22:30).

The intercessor is the true man of power because he moves God. That is real power! Elijah saved a nation through intercession, not through preaching. When God looks for a man who can avert His wrath against a people, those people are beyond preaching. He seeks the only person who can remedy the situation: an intercessor.

Although perhaps not clever or brilliant or gifted, the intercessor does have a prepared and willing heart. Preparation not only means a heart that has been cleansed by Christ's blood but also purged of self-orientation, which competes with achieving God's will through intercessory prayer. Because the intercessor must be morally able to stand before God, a holy character is required. This man or woman's effectiveness, usefulness, and ultimately fruitfulness depends upon personal holiness.

The morally able intercessor can be filled with the Spirit and walk in the Spirit, knowing by the Spirit the will of God. Interceding is not simply getting answers from God or knowing certain things about prayer. It is a matter of being filled with the Spirit. That is the issue. Without the Spirit's revelation of the will of God, the intercessor's prayers don't count in the great battle for souls.

Personal Reflections:

Jesus, Master, Whose I Am

Jesus, Master, Whose I am,
Purchased Thine alone to be,
By Thy blood, O spotless Lamb,
Shed so willingly for me.
Let my heart be all Thine own,
Let me live to Thee alone.

Other lords have long held sway;
Now, Thy name alone to bear,
Thy dear voice alone obey,
Is my daily, hourly, prayer:
Whom have I in heaven but Thee?
Nothing else my joy can be.

Jesus, Master, wilt Thou use
One who owes Thee more than all?
As Thou wilt! I would not choose;
Only let me hear Thy call.
Jesus, let me always be,
In Thy service, glad and free.

      Francis Ridley Havergal

Reflections on Prayer

Day 29 CHARACTERISTICS OF INTERCESSORS

And I sought for a man among them, that should make up the hedge, and stand in the gap before me for the land, that I should not destroy it...(Ezekiel 22:30).

When God puts His defenses around an individual or a people or a work, He calls this a hedge. The devil tries to break down that hedge to destroy. If the hedge is broken, someone must stand against the enemy's onslaughts. God looks for an intercessor who can "stand in the gap," which is an image for intercession.

The intercessor must be a certain kind of man; otherwise, he's not going to be able to make up the gap. He is *compassionate*, identifying with the needs of the people or person. This is a man or woman who comes before the Lord as if the needs were their own. Intercessors compassionately identify with others.

The intercessor is also *consistent*. He doesn't give up until the answers come. Moses stood before the Lord for 40 days and 40 nights without giving up. The intercessor will see lives changed in answer to their consistent prayers.

Above and beyond all else, the intercessor is *concerned* for the glory of God. That is the dominating desire of his heart.

Day 29 CHARACTERISTICS OF INTERCESSORS
(continued)

What does God see in your character? Do you compassionately identify with others? Is there consistency in persisting until God's will prevails? How far are you willing to go? Are you willing to get to the point where nothing really counts except the glory of God?

Day 30 ANSWERED PRAYER

And whatsoever we ask, we receive of him, because we keep his commandments, and do those things that are pleasing in his sight
(I John 3:22).

We live on a little mud ball called Earth. It's just a little speck in the universe, and ours is just one universe among countless universes. The eternal, omnipresent, omnipotent God has a throne. Have you meditated on the fact that you can touch that throne? You can actually move the One who sits upon that exalted throne. To do so is not a matter of your earnestness. It is a matter of your obedience, the surrender of your will to the will of God as revealed in His Word.

Whom does God hear? The man who keeps the Lord's commandments is heard. This man comes with confidence before the throne of God because he not only has access but also is welcomed.

You have access, but are you welcomed by the Father? If you listen to God's commandments, He listens to your prayers. If you keep His commandments, doing those things that are pleasing in His sight, your prayers will be answered. This is the testimony of the Word of God.

Prayer Journal

Also From Joseph Carroll

How To Worship Jesus Christ

This book focuses on the essential of worship, the most important element of prayer. C. S. Lewis confirms that worship is key: "...it is in the process of worship that God communicates His presence to men."

David's ruling passion was to dwell in God's house to meditate and behold His beauty. The Apostle Paul's passion was to know Him through intimate fellowship. It is through worship that one shares the innermost secrets of the heart of God.

In this volume, believers find inspiration as worship is defined, hindrances are outlined, and requirements are explained. Chapters then suggest practical ways to develop a life of worship.

Many testimonies of changed lives offer proof that God delights to foster greater love and deeper intimacy through worship.

History Of EI

Training believers to live like Christ, for Christ, out of the riches of Christ, anywhere in the world.

Joseph Carroll founded The Evangelical Institute (EI) in 1967 on 50 acres of farmland at the base of Paris Mountain in Greenville, South Carolina. He envisioned the need for a Bible school with a new emphasis. Contact with missionaries through his itinerant conference ministry in the Far East convinced him that a Christian life or ministry that did not recognize the primacy of prayer and worship was destined to fail. So, EI was established to instill foundational principles of the Christian life.

EI could be described as an evangelical, non-denominational fellowship holding to the fundamental beliefs that define biblical Christianity. The aim of our one or two-year program is to bring each student into a vital, enduring fellowship with Jesus Christ through a life of prayer, faith, obedience to God's Word, and service. We endeavor to create an environment in which an understanding of God's ways is taught to seeking hearts and a deep love for the Lord is nurtured.

Over the years, the Bible school and conference center developed as the Lord not only provided land and buildings but also the fellow workers necessary to teach classes and coordinate conference meetings.

Since the first class of 1972, hundreds of students from the United States and internationals from more than 35 different countries have found their way to Greenville to see the life of faith lived before them and to begin to walk that path themselves.

Many of our graduates are now involved in missions all over the world. Other graduates pastor churches and are involved in national mission projects, while many more serve the Lord faithfully in local churches.

EI School of Biblical Training
700 North Parker Road
Greenville, SC 29609
www.eibibleschool.org

Made in the USA
Coppell, TX
12 March 2021

51645587R00075